THE REVENGE
OF THE BABY-SAT

Other Books by Bill Watterson

Calvin and Hobbes
Something Under the Bed Is Drooling
Yukon Ho!
Weirdos From Another Planet!

Treasury Collections

The Essential Calvin and Hobbes
The Calvin and Hobbes Lazy Sunday Book
The Authoritative Calvin and Hobbes

THE REVENGE OF THE BABY-SAT

A Calvin and Hobbes Collection by Bill Watterson

Andrews and McMeel
A Universal Press Syndicate Company
Kansas City • New York

Calvin and Hobbes is distributed internationally by Universal Press Syndicate.

 For information write Andrews and McMeel, a Universal Press Syndicate Company, 4900 Main Street, Kansas City, Missouri 64112.

ISBN: 0-8362-1866-3

Library of Congress Catalog Card Number: 90-85466

Printed on recycled paper.

10

13

19

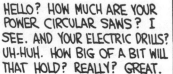

39

40

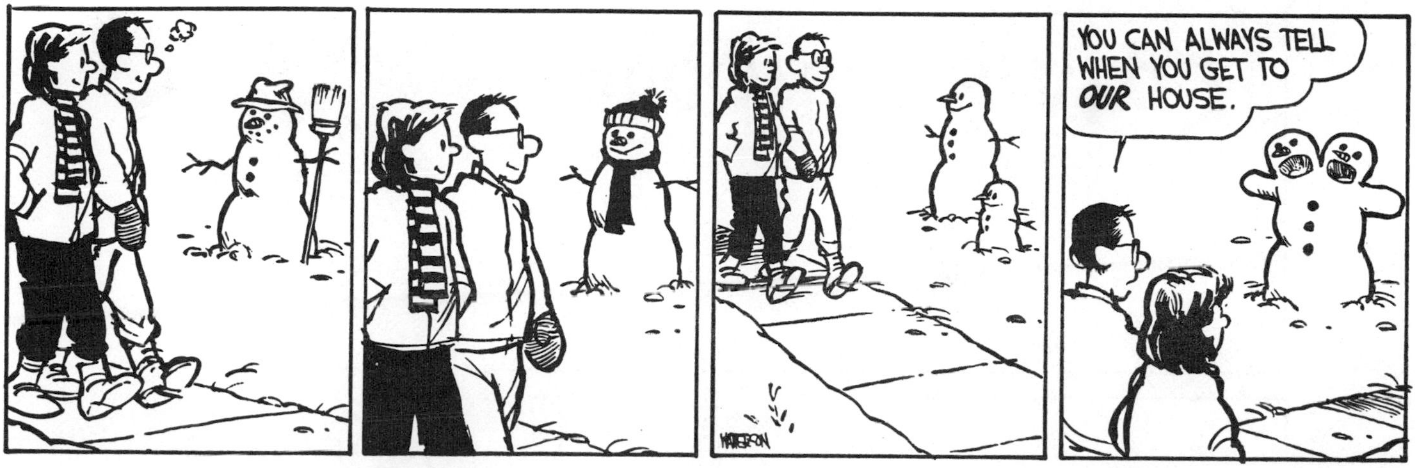
YOU CAN ALWAYS TELL WHEN YOU GET TO ***OUR*** HOUSE.

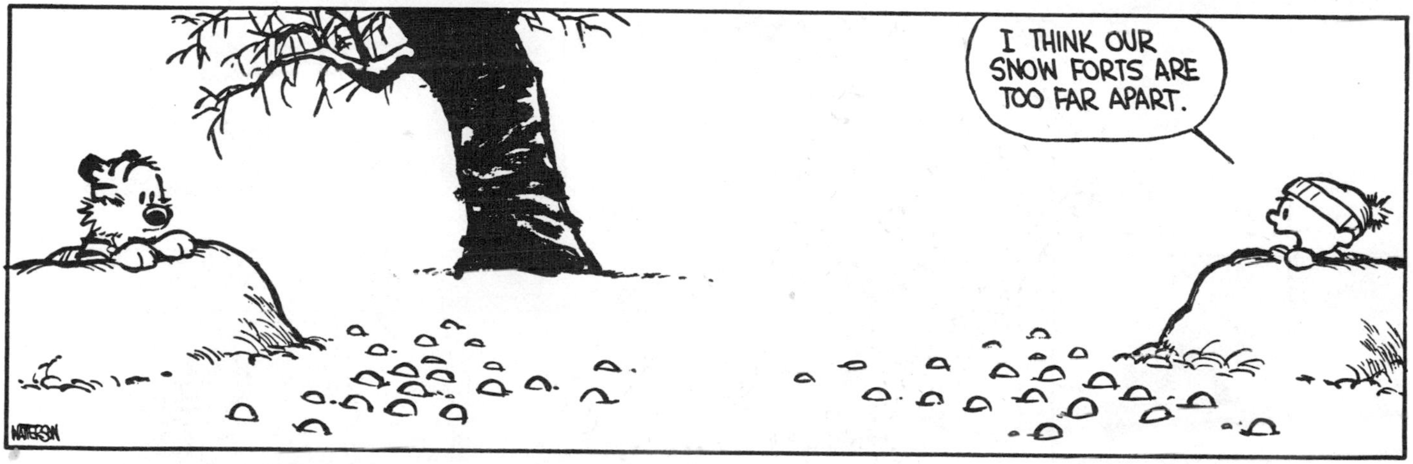
I THINK OUR SNOW FORTS ARE TOO FAR APART.

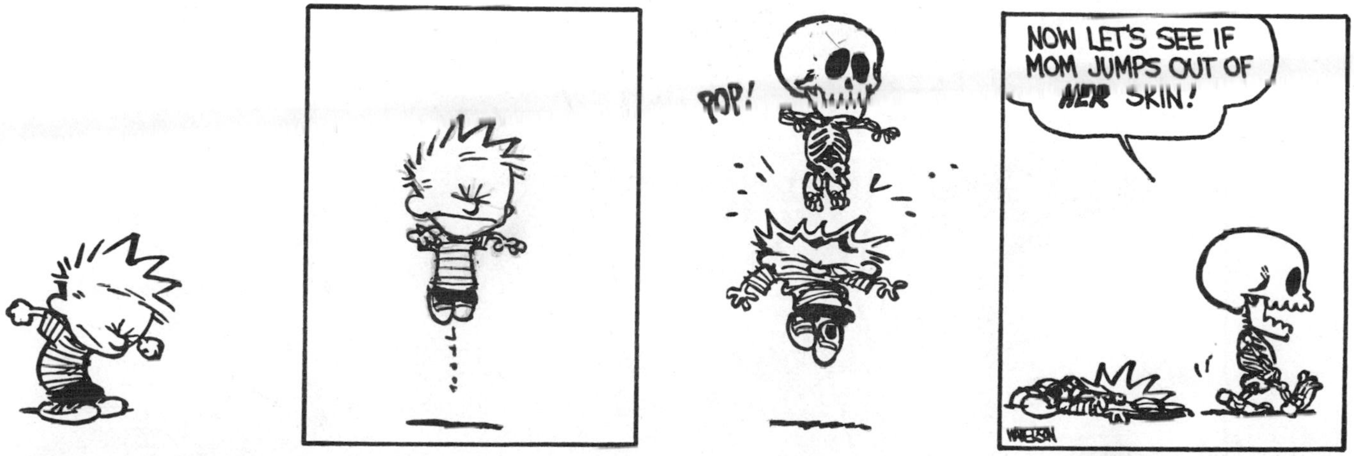
POP!
NOW LET'S SEE IF MOM JUMPS OUT OF ***HER*** SKIN!

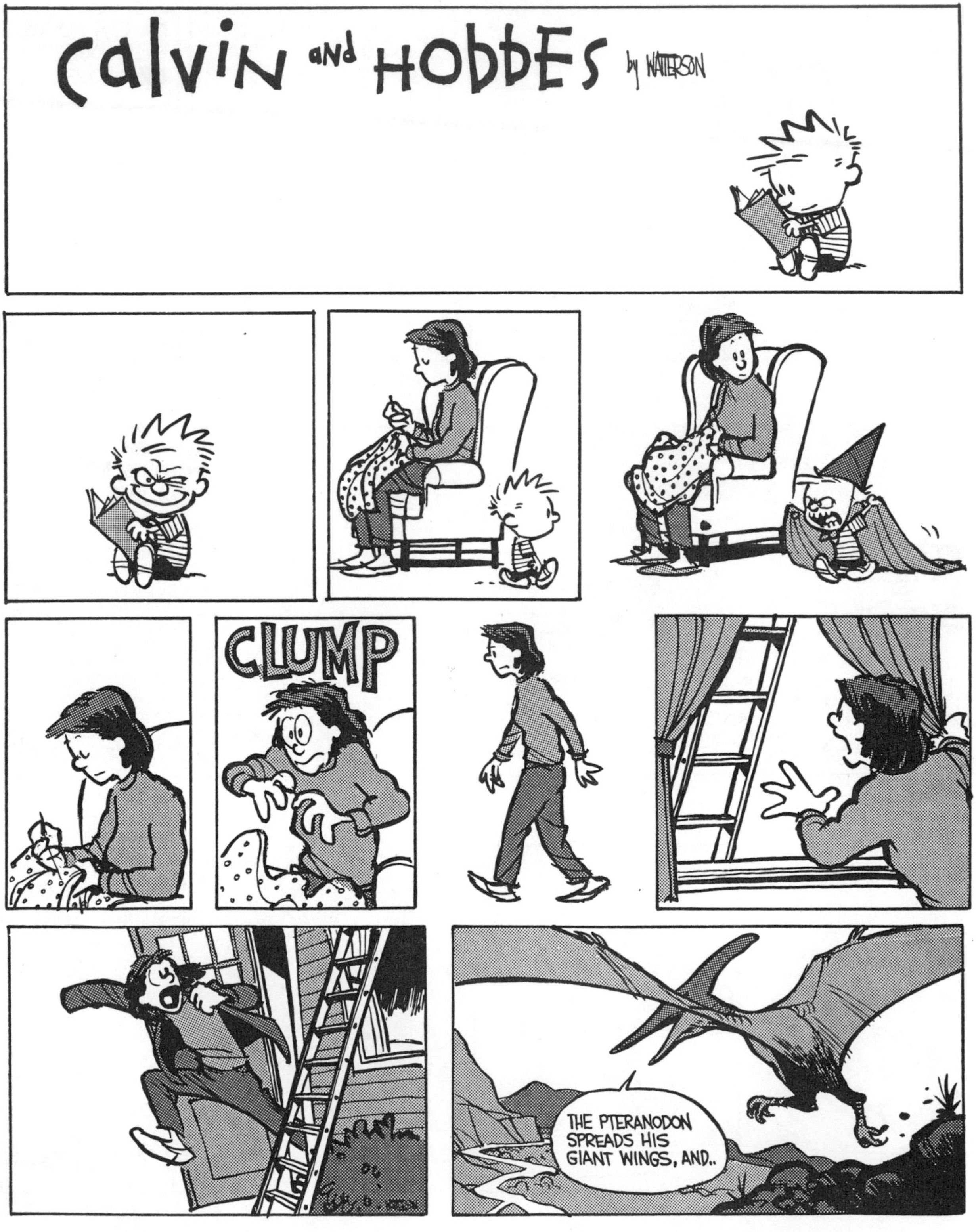
Calvin and HOBBES
by WATTERSON
CLUMP
THE PTERANODON SPREADS HIS GIANT WINGS, AND..

43

48

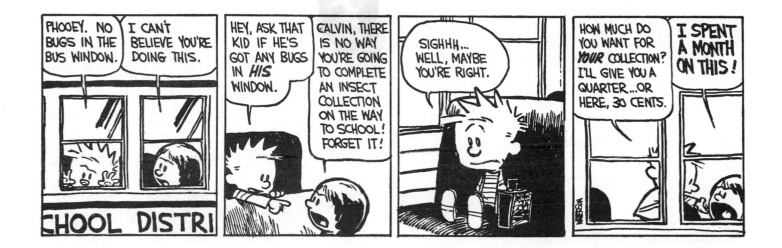

PHOOEY. NO BUGS IN THE BUS WINDOW.

I CAN'T BELIEVE YOU'RE DOING THIS.

CHOOL DISTRI

HEY, ASK THAT KID IF HE'S GOT ANY BUGS IN HIS WINDOW.

CALVIN, THERE IS NO WAY YOU'RE GOING TO COMPLETE AN INSECT COLLECTION ON THE WAY TO SCHOOL! FORGET IT!

SIGHHH... WELL, MAYBE YOU'RE RIGHT.

HOW MUCH DO YOU WANT FOR YOUR COLLECTION? I'LL GIVE YOU A QUARTER...OR HERE, 30 CENTS.

I SPENT A MONTH ON THIS!

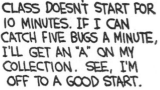

HEY, HERE'S A WORM! WORMS ARE BUGS, AREN'T THEY?

EWW GROSS, CALVIN! THAT'S BEEN FLOATING IN A PUDDLE FOR DAYS.

CLASS DOESN'T START FOR 10 MINUTES. IF I CAN CATCH FIVE BUGS A MINUTE, I'LL GET AN "A" ON MY COLLECTION. SEE, I'M OFF TO A GOOD START.

FIVE BUGS A MINUTE ?! YOU'RE OUT OF YOUR MIND.

HERE'S ANOTHER ALREADY.

THAT'S A LITTLE BALL OF LINT!

LIKE I'M SURE THE TEACHER'S GOING TO LOOK REAL CLOSE AT EVERY HAIRY BUG IN 30 KIDS' COLLECTIONS!

RINNGGGG

THERE'S THE BELL. WE'VE GOT TO GO TO CLASS.

RATS. I DIDN'T GET 50 BUGS YET.

WHAT DO YOU HAVE?

ONE DROWNED WORM, A PIECE OF FUZZY LINT THAT LOOKS LIKE A BUG, A LIVE ANT, AND A SMASHED FLY.

WELL, IF YOU LABEL THEM SCIENTIFICALLY IN THE NEXT 30 SECONDS, MAYBE YOU'LL GET AN "F+."

WE'VE GOT TO LABEL THESE TOO ?!? I WAS JUST GOING TO PUT THEM ALL IN AN ENVELOPE.

ACTUALLY, I DON'T THINK THERE'S ANY WAY YOU'LL GET AN "F+."

FOR ALL THIS WORK, I'D BETTER AT LEAST GET A "D."

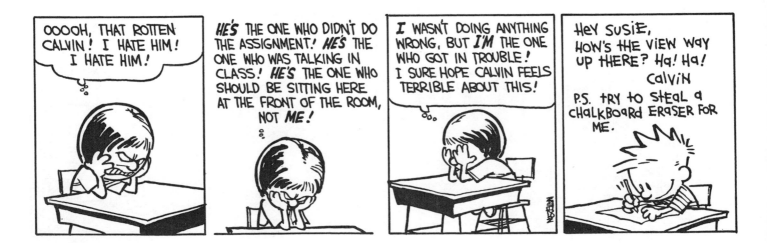

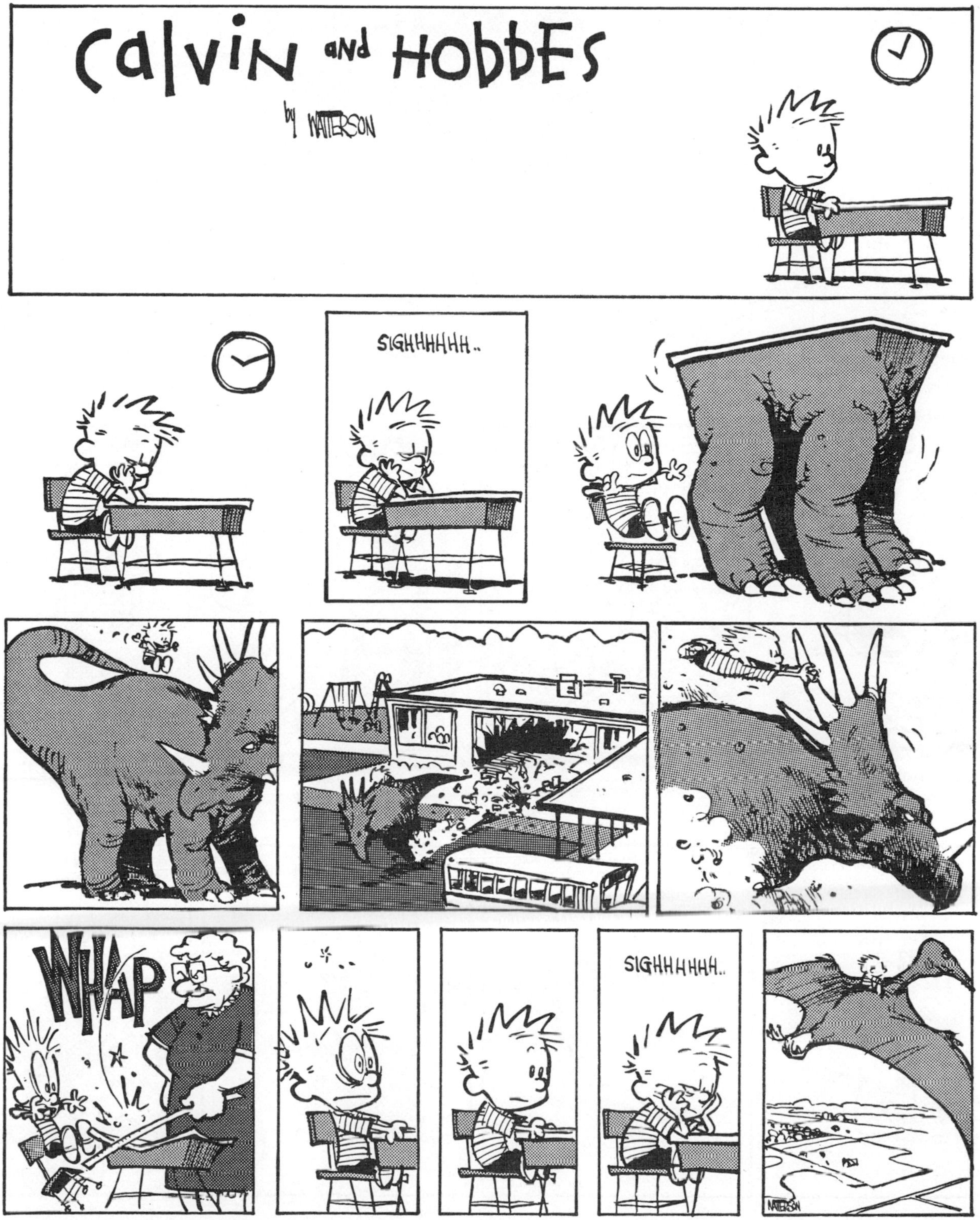
Calvin and HOBBES
by WATTERSON
SIGHHHHHH..
WHAP
SIGHHHHHH..
WATTERSON

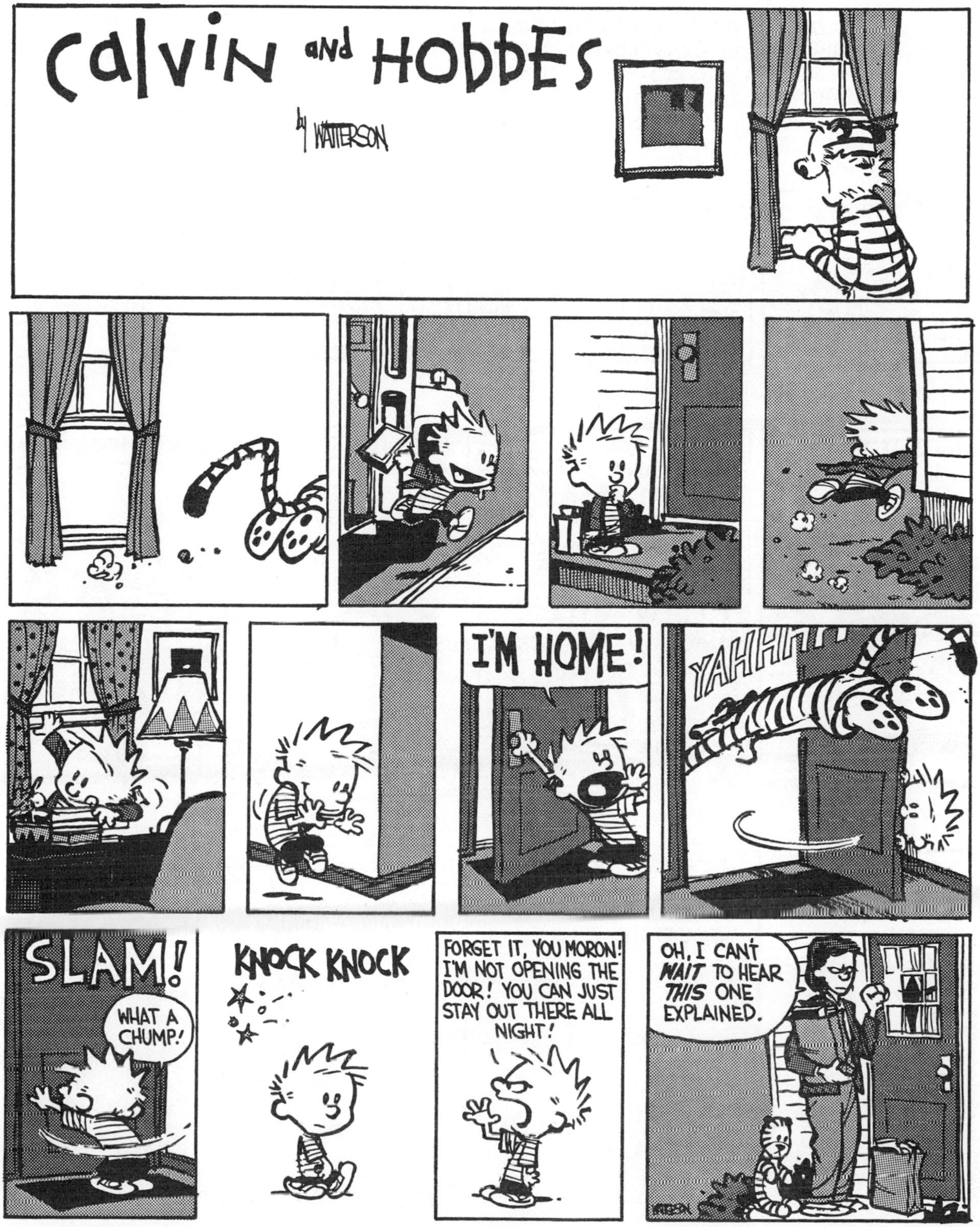
Calvin and HOBBES
by WATTERSON
I'M HOME!
YAHHHH
SLAM!
WHAT A CHUMP!
KNOCK KNOCK
FORGET IT, YOU MORON! I'M NOT OPENING THE DOOR! YOU CAN JUST STAY OUT THERE ALL NIGHT!
OH, I CAN'T WAIT TO HEAR THIS ONE EXPLAINED.

WELL, AT LEAST WE WEREN'T HOME WHEN OUR HOUSE WAS BROKEN INTO. NO ONE WAS HURT. WE'RE ALL TOGETHER AND OK.

WE LOST A FEW OF OUR NICE THINGS, BUT THINGS DON'T MATTER MUCH REALLY.

IT'S HARD TO BELIEVE HOW OFTEN WE FORGET THAT.

CAN I BE EXCUSED NOW?

YOU DIDN'T FINISH YOUR DINNER.

WELL, I DIDN'T LIKE IT VERY MUCH, AND THERE'S THIS TV SHOW I WANT TO WATCH, SO...

OUR TV WAS STOLEN, REMEMBER?

GOSH, I GUESS I'LL EAT MY ASPARAGUS, DO MY HOMEWORK, AND GO STRAIGHT TO BED, THEN.

AND WE'RE SO PROUD OF HOW YOU HANDLE ADVERSITY.

THIS IS WHERE OUR TELEVISION USED TO BE.

BUT WE DON'T HAVE A TV ANYMORE. NOW WE HAVE A BLANK WALL TO WATCH.

SO HERE I AM, NOT BEING ENTERTAINED.

A POINTLESS EXISTENCE, HUH?

I MEAN, THE WALL IS EVEN PLAIN OLD *WHITE!*

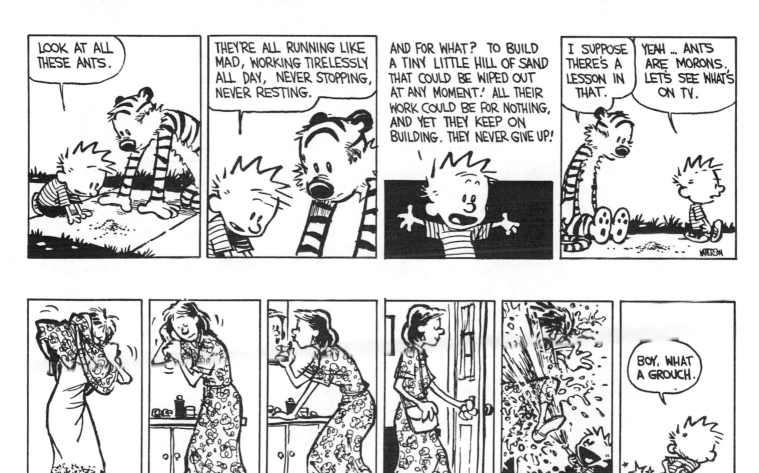

IT'S JULY ALREADY! OH NO! OH NO!

WHAT HAPPENED TO JUNE?! SUMMER VACATION IS SLIPPING THROUGH OUR FINGERS LIKE GRAINS OF SAND!

IT'S GOING TOO FAST! WE'VE GOT TO HOARD OUR FREEDOM AND HAVE MORE FUN! TIME RUSHES ON! HELP! HELP!

I DON'T THINK I WANT TO BE HERE AT THE END OF AUGUST.

AAUGH! IT'S A HALF-HOUR LATER THAN IT WAS HALF AN HOUR AGO! RUN! RUN!

MOM TOOK ME TO THE LIBRARY TODAY, DAD.

THAT'S NICE. DID YOU GET OUT A BOOK?

YEP. IT'S GREAT! I HAD NO IDEA BOOKS COULD BE SO MUCH FUN.

AND YOU'LL LEARN THINGS, TOO.

I'LL SAY! MY BOOK SAYS THAT THIS ONE WASP LAYS ITS EGG ON A SPIDER, SO WHEN THE EGG HATCHES, THE LARVA EATS THE SPIDER, SAVING THE VITAL ORGANS FOR LAST, SO THE SPIDER STAYS ALIVE WHILE IT'S BEING DEVOURED!

GROSS, HUH?

ISN'T THERE A STREET CORNER WHERE HE COULD HANG OUT INSTEAD?

AND COLOR PICTURES, TOO! WANT TO SEE 'EM?

I'M DESTINED FOR GREATNESS, I JUST KNOW IT. "CALVIN THE GREAT," THEY'LL CALL ME.

AND THINK HOW LUCKY YOU'LL BE! YOU'LL GET TO TELL EVERYONE HOW YOU KNEW ME AS A KID! WHAT A PRIVILEGE!

IN FACT, ALL THE PAPERS AND MAGAZINES WILL PROBABLY WANT TO INTERVIEW YOU TO FIND OUT WHAT I'M REALLY LIKE.

AND BOY, WILL YOU HAVE TO COUGH UP TO KEEP ME QUIET.

AND WHAT'S THAT SUPPOSED TO MEAN?!

WUM WUM WUM

HOW'S IT GOING?

FINE. CLOSE THE LID. EVERYTHING STOPS WHEN YOU OPEN IT.

I WISH *MY* BATHTUB HAD AN AGITATOR.

CALVIN, WILL YOU GATHER THE TRASH, PLEASE?

GATHER THE *TRASH*?!? WHAT AM I, YOUR PERSONAL *SLAVE*?! WHY CAN'T *YOU* DO IT?

FINE, I WILL. AND *YOU* CAN START WASHING YOUR *OWN* CLOTHES, AND FIXING YOUR *OWN* MEALS, AND PICKING UP YOUR *OWN* TOYS, AND MAKING YOUR *OWN* BED, AND CLEANING UP YOUR *OWN* MESSES, DAY AFTER DAY AFTER *DAY!*

SOME WOMEN JUST WEREN'T MEANT TO BE MOTHERS.

WHENEVER I COOK AN EGG, I LIKE TO SEE HOW HIGH I CAN CRACK IT ABOVE THE SKILLET.

THEN I AIM WITH JUST ONE EYE OPEN, SO I DON'T HAVE ANY DEPTH PERCEPTION. IT'S PRETTY HARD THAT WAY.

SEE, THE SECRET TO HAVING FUN IN LIFE IS TO MAKE LITTLE CHALLENGES FOR YOURSELF.

CRIKK

LIKE THE CHALLENGE OF EXPLAINING THE STOVE AND FLOOR TO YOUR MOM?

RATS. SEE IF THERE'S ANOTHER CARTON IN THE FRIDGE, WILL YA?

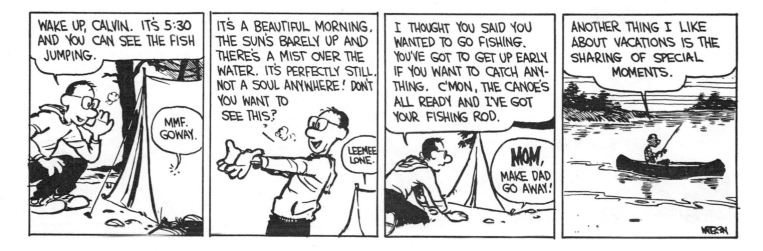

105

Panel 1:
OFF TO WORK, EH, DAD?
YEP.

Panel 2:
IT SURE IS A NICE DAY. THE KIND OF DAY JUST MADE FOR SITTING UNDER A TREE AND READING A GOOD NOVEL COVER TO COVER, DON'T YOU THINK?

Panel 3:
TOO BAD THAT'S A LUXURY AT YOUR AGE. WELL, MAYBE YOU CAN DO IT WHEN YOU'RE 65. I'M SURE YOU'LL BE THAT OLD BEFORE YOU KNOW IT. ENJOY YOUR DAY AT WORK.

Panel 4:
DAD SURE IS SURLY IN THE MORNINGS.

Panel 5:
YOU KNOW WHAT'S WEIRD? I DON'T REMEMBER MUCH OF ANYTHING UNTIL I WAS THREE YEARS OLD.

Panel 6:
HALF OF MY LIFE IS A COMPLETE BLANK! I MUST'VE BEEN BRAINWASHED!

Panel 7:
GOOD HEAVENS, WHAT KIND OF SICKO WOULD BRAINWASH AN INFANT?! AND WHAT DID I KNOW THAT SOMEONE WANTED ME TO FORGET??

Panel 8:
BOY, AM I MYSTERIOUS.
I SEEM TO RECALL YOU SPENT MOST OF THE TIME BURPING UP.

Panel 9:
MOM! THERE'S A BIG HORSEFLY ON THE BACK OF YOUR HEAD! DON'T MOVE! I'LL GET IT!

Panel 11:
IS IT STILL THERE? YOU DIDN'T MOVE, DID YOU?
GET AWAY FROM ME!

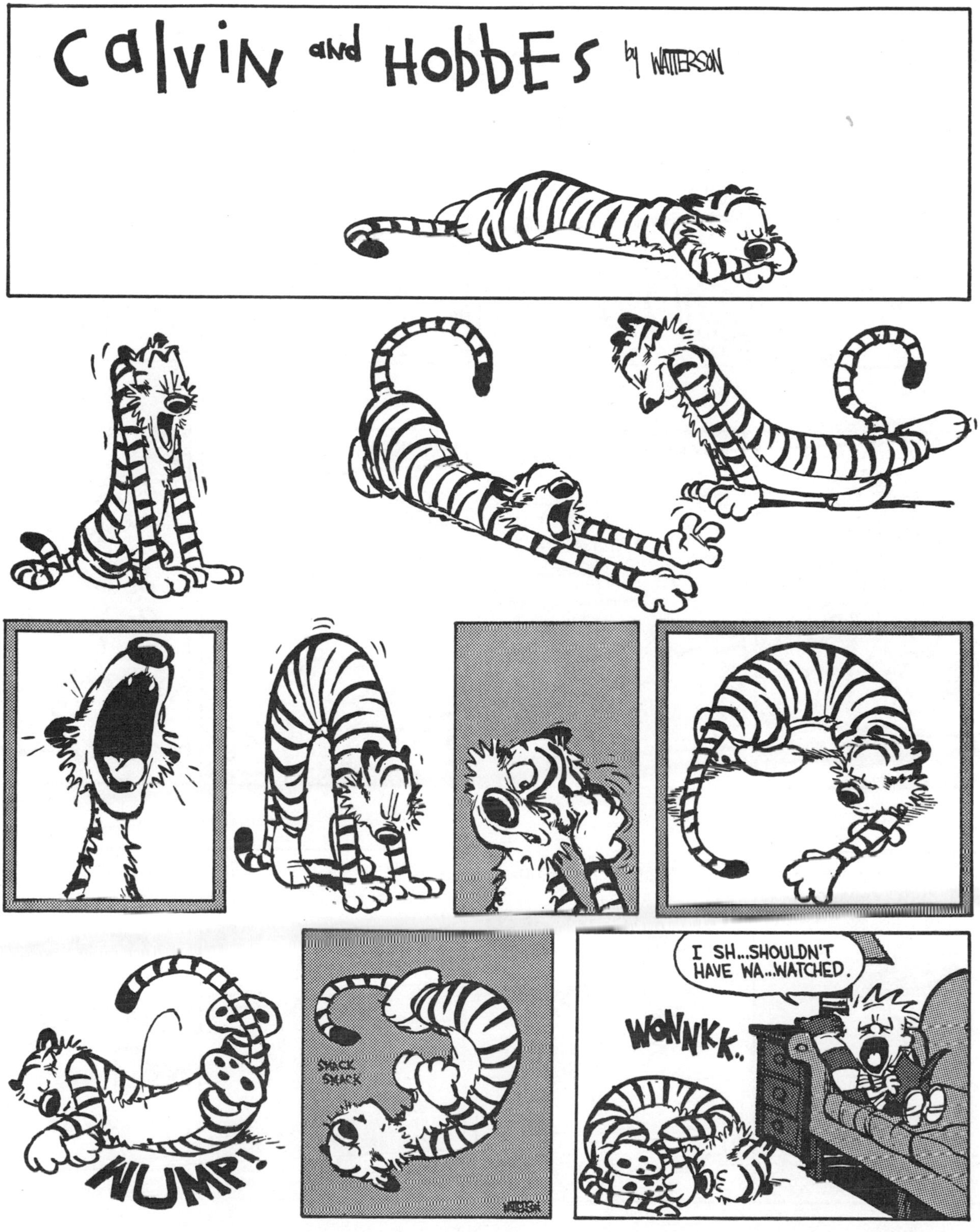

Calvin and HOBBES
by WATTERSON
NUMP!
SMACK SMACK
WONNKK..
I SH...SHOULDN'T HAVE WA...WATCHED.

Row 1

CALVIN THE HUMMINGBIRD ZIPS BY WITH A LOUD WHIR!

ALTHOUGH SMALL, HE PUTS OUT TREMENDOUS ENERGY. TO HOVER, HIS WINGS BEAT HUNDREDS OF TIMES EACH SECOND!

WHAT FUELS THIS INCREDIBLE METABOLISM? CONCENTRATED SUGAR WATER! HE DRINKS HALF HIS WEIGHT A DAY!

...PREFERABLY LOADED WITH CAFFEINE.

ARE YOU DRINKING MORE SODA POP?!

SLURRPP

Row 2

"ONCE UPON A TIME THERE WAS..."

HOLD IT.

WHAT'S THE MATTER?

HAS THIS BOOK BEEN A BEST SELLER? HAS THE AUTHOR WON A PULITZER? DID THE NEW YORK TIMES LIKE IT?

I ONLY WANT STORIES THAT COME HIGHLY RECOMMENDED. ARE THERE ANY LAUDATORY QUOTES ON THE DUST JACKET?

AHEM..."ONCE UPON A TIME THERE WAS A NOISY KID WHO STARTED GOING TO BED WITHOUT A STORY."

HAS THIS BOOK BEEN MADE INTO A MOVIE? COULD WE BE WATCHING THIS ON VIDEO?

Row 3

WHAT ARE YOU DOING?

I'M PRACTICING MY SNEERS.

THERE'S NOTHING LIKE A GOOD SNEER TO DRY UP CONVERSATION. HOW'S MINE LOOK?

AWFUL!

THANKS. WITH THIS SNEER, I HOPE TO BE AN UNBEARABLE BURDEN AT ANY SOCIAL OCCASION.

THAT WILL GIVE YOU A REAL HEAD START ON BEING A TEEN-AGER.

I KNOW! IT'S LIKE GETTING SEVEN EXTRA YEARS!

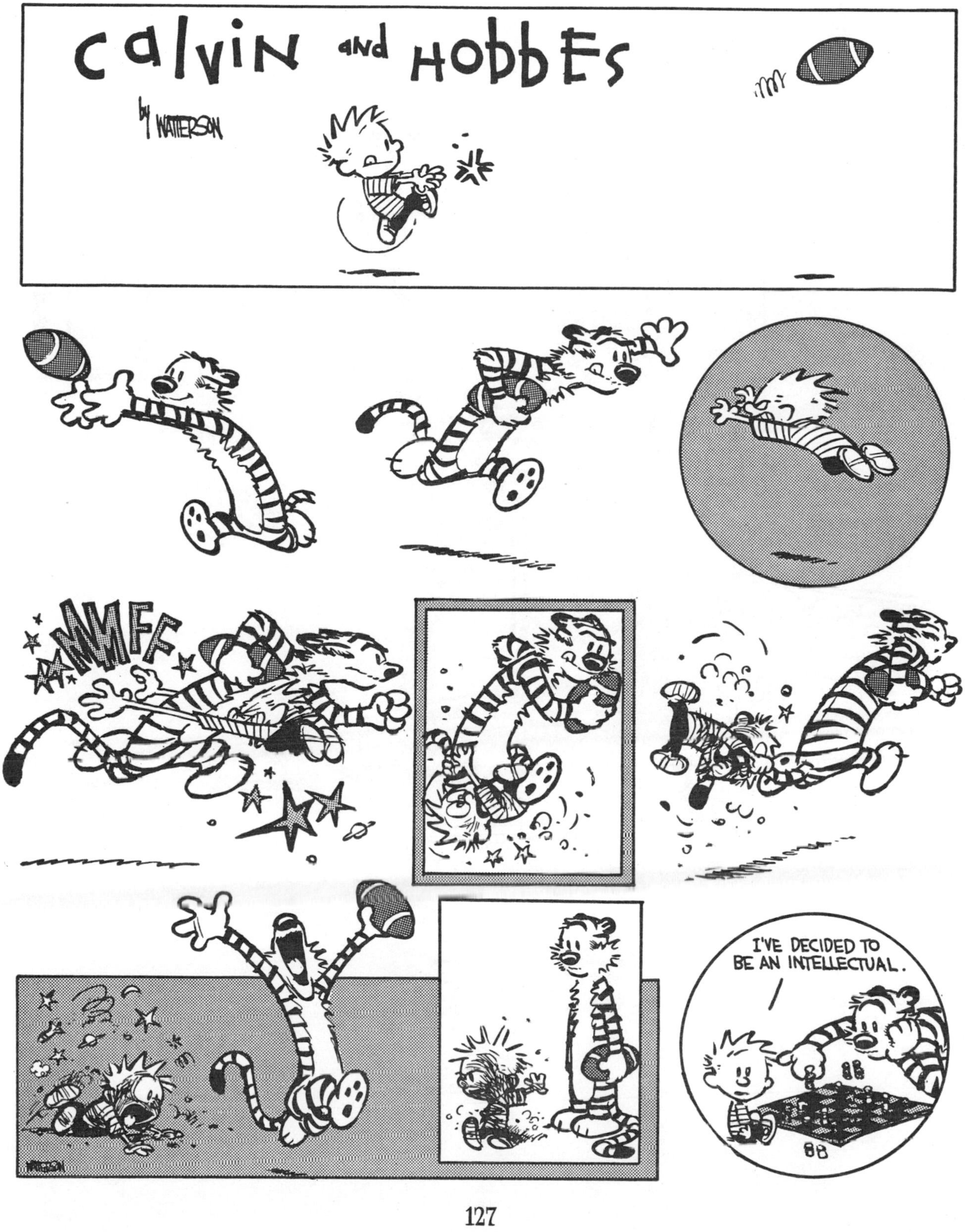
CALVIN AND HOBBES
by WATTERSON
NMFF
I'VE DECIDED TO BE AN INTELLECTUAL.

The End